STATHEAD SPORTS

STATHEAD
BASEBALL
How Data Changed the Sport

by Eric Braun

COMPASS POINT BOOKS
a capstone imprint

Stathead Sports is published
by Compass Point Books, a Capstone imprint
1710 Roe Crest Drive, North Mankato, Minnesota 56003
www.mycapstone.com

Library of Congress Cataloging-in-Publication Data is available on the Library
of Congress website.
ISBN 978-1-5435-1449-0 (library binding)
ISBN 978-1-5435-1453-7 (paperback)
ISBN 978-1-5435-1457-5 (eBook PDF)

Editorial Credits
Nick Healy, editor; Terri Poburka, designer; Eric Gohl, media researcher;
Laura Manthe, production specialist

Photo Credits
AP Photo: Bizuayehu Tesfaye, 17; Dreamstime: Jerry Coli, 14, 16, 32, Ron Hoff,
27; Getty Images: Focus On Sport, 21, Icon SMI/Daniel Gluskoter, 22, Icon
Sportswire, 5, Icon Sportswire/Nick Wosika, 28, Larry Goren, 24, Mike Stobe, 38,
Post-Dispatch/J.B. Forbes, 30, Stephen Dunn, 12, The Sporting News, 11; Library
of Congress: 8, 18; New York Public Library: 10; Newscom: Icon Sportswire/
Nick Wosika, 28, Larry Goren, 24, Post-Dispatch/J.B. Forbes, 30, UPI/Brian Kersey,
43, UPI/Pat Benic, 36, USA Today Sports/Dennis Wierzbicki, cover, USA Today
Sports/Tommy Gilligan, 4, ZUMA Press/Frank Gunn, 7, ZUMA Press/Matt Masin,
44, ZUMA Press/Mike Greene, 35; Shutterstock: Danai Khampiranon, back cover,
40, Photo Works, 33

Design Elements: Shutterstock

Printed in the United States of America.
PA017

TABLE OF CONTENTS

Introduction
HOW A STAT RUINED ONE TEAM'S SEASON 4

Chapter 1
BASEBALL HAS ALWAYS LOVED NUMBERS 8

Chapter 2
A NEW WAY OF THINKING ABOUT STATS 14

Chapter 3
SMALL CHANGES TAKE HOLD 22

Chapter 4
ADVANCED STATISTICS GO MAINSTREAM 30

Chapter 5
THE NEXT FRONTIER IN STATS 38

Stat Glossary 46
Read More 47
Internet Sites 47
Index 48

HOW A STAT RUINED ONE TEAM'S SEASON

▲ Reliever Zach Britton saved many wins for the O's but never got a chance to pitch in a crucial postseason game.

Zach Britton of the Baltimore Orioles had one of the best seasons for a relief pitcher—or for any pitcher—in modern history. In 2016, Britton converted all 47 of his save opportunities. He finished with a squint-to-see-it 0.54 earned run average (ERA). He was so good, he came in fourth place in American League Cy Young voting, rare for a reliever.

So when the Orioles entered the postseason, they had a powerful weapon at their disposal. In the playoffs every out is precious. It is comforting for a manager to know he has a guy who makes collecting high-pressure outs look as easy as collecting baseball cards.

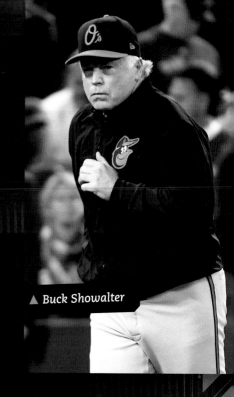

▲ Buck Showalter

Good thing, too, because their wild-card game against the Toronto Blue Jays was high-pressure from the start. One game, winner takes all. Win and advance. Lose and go home.

When the Jays tied the game 2-2 in the fifth inning, Orioles manager Buck Showalter went to his bullpen for the first time. As the game crept toward the late innings, it remained tied. The pressure increased. Every out became more important than the last one.

In the bottom of the ninth inning, Showalter made what many considered a blunder. That inning was by far the most dangerous for Baltimore all night. Toronto was sending its three best hitters to the plate. If they scored, the game was over. Baltimore wouldn't get a chance to make a comeback.

But instead of bringing in his best pitcher, Zach Britton, the O's manager called on Brad Brach. Brach had a rocky inning but escaped without giving up a run. Blunder or not, the Orioles were still alive.

Sidearmer Darren O'Day got the Orioles through the tenth. Then, with one out in the eleventh, the top of the Blue Jays order was coming up again. This moment was even more dangerous than the ninth. And Showalter went to his bullpen for . . . Ubaldo Jiminez.

Jiminez was a good pitcher, but he was no Britton. He gave up two quick singles. Then Edwin Encarnacion lumbered to the plate. Encarnacion was a one-man wrecking crew who had 42 home runs in the regular season.

Showalter called for time. He wanted to talk it over with his pitcher. The fans at Rogers Center in Toronto were screaming in anticipation. If ever there was a time to bring in your stopper, this was it. But once again, Showalter chose to save his closer for later.

Showalter walked back to the dugout, leaving Jiminez toeing the rubber. At the plate, Encarnacion waved his big bat in the air. Jiminez reared back and threw his pitch.

Kaboom!

Encarnacion sent it screaming into the stands. While the home team celebrated its victory on the field, the best reliever in baseball sat in the visitors' bullpen. Britton was helpless to do anything but watch.

Showalter was known as a smart manager. In his 18-year career he had a winning percentage of .521 and won Manager of the Year three times. But after the game, he admitted that he'd been saving Britton. The manager was waiting until his team could get a lead, when the closer could seal things with a save. As the team's closer, that was Britton's job.

▲ The Jays' Edwin Encarnacion hit a walk-off homer as the Orioles' best reliever sat in the bullpen.

Showalter let a statistic (the save) influence his decision-making. He had been too focused on keeping Britton available for a save situation. As a result, he left a lesser pitcher on the hill in a dangerous situation.

Statistics are a wonderful part of baseball. They help us understand the stories that take place. They help us appreciate just how good a certain player or team is. They help players prepare to face their opponents. And they help managers make decisions.

But statistics can be deceiving too. That's why baseball analysts keep working to create better stats and better ways to use stats.

Baseball analysis has experienced a major shift over the past generation. For a long time, the only numbers considered important in baseball were the "baseball card" stats. Those include batting average, runs batted in (RBI), home runs, stolen bases, and pitcher wins.

Today we have dozens of stats that are better, more precise, more predictive, and more useful than those old-school numbers. And more are on the way.

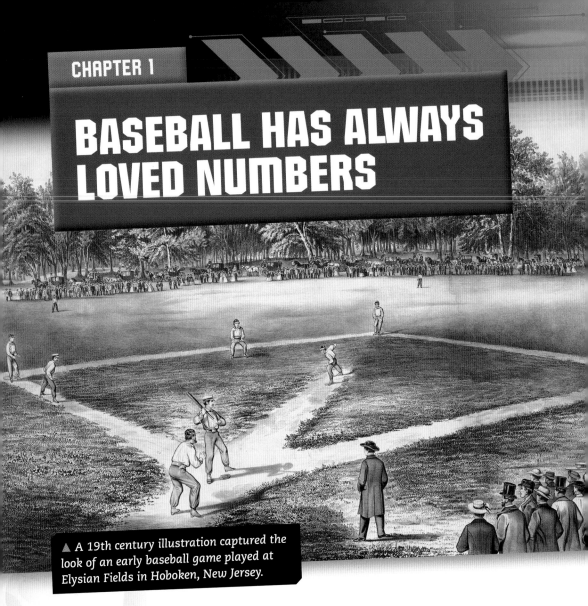

CHAPTER 1

BASEBALL HAS ALWAYS LOVED NUMBERS

▲ A 19th century illustration captured the look of an early baseball game played at Elysian Fields in Hoboken, New Jersey.

One afternoon in the fall of 1856, a *New York Times* reporter named Henry Chadwick was covering a cricket game at Elysian Fields in West Hoboken, New Jersey. Chadwick was an Englishman who'd come to the United States nearly twenty years earlier. He had seen "base ball" played before. It had never much captured his attention. He considered it less interesting than cricket, which was a traditional game of the English.

But as he walked across the park that day, he saw a game of baseball being played. Two New York teams, the Gotham and Eagles clubs, were squaring off. The players moved quickly, and the action was more vigorous than in cricket. Baseball had energy, and the men played it aggressively. Chadwick was fascinated. Baseball seemed to him to be a particularly American sport. It seemed well suited to the people of the relatively young nation.

As he said, "Americans do not care to dawdle over a sleep-inspiring game, all through the heat of a June or July day. What they do they want to do in a hurry. In baseball all is lightning; every action is as swift as a seabird's flight."

Covering the Game

It was lucky for the game of baseball that Chadwick happened to walk past that day. From then on, he made it his goal to promote it as the American pastime. He wrote about the sport for several publications. He reported on games and summarized the results.

Baseball did receive news coverage before Chadwick came along. Back in October 1845, three baseball games had been played between two New York teams. Their scorebook still exists in the New York Public Library. The first games to be recorded in a box score appeared in the *New York Morning News* on October 22 of that year. The box score provided a simple and elegant summary of the ballgame. It noted how many times each player had scored a run and how many times he'd made an out.

Chadwick's work greatly advanced news coverage and use of statistics. In 1859, he created the modern box score. He also became the first to regularly record and publish statistics such as runs, hits, put-outs, assists, errors, and strikeouts, which he represented with a "K" in the box score. He also created the batting average statistic, and he introduced the idea of earned and unearned runs. Since newspapers rarely published photos then, the best way to really show the game was through numbers.

Along with his box scores, Chadwick wrote detailed game descriptions. Readers could follow the sport even if they couldn't get out to the ballpark to watch it. Soon Chadwick was compiling stats for whole teams and seasons in *The Beadle's Dime Base Ball Player*, which he edited yearly starting in 1860. For the first time, fans could compare players' and teams' statistics.

◀ The scorecard from an 1846 game is part of a collection at the New York Public Library.

Chadwick's work made baseball more popular at the end of the century. Baseball fans loved reading game recaps and poring over stats. Stats became so important that some fans and journalists complained that players cared more about their numbers than their team winning.

▲ Henry Chadwick

Traditional Stats

The game of baseball changed a lot during this time. Originally pitchers just tossed the ball underhand to hitters. They didn't try to fool them or fire the ball past them. Fielders didn't use gloves. To get a runner out, they would throw the ball at him. The runner was out if he got pegged. By the end of the 1800s, though, the game looked mostly like the game we know today. And the statistics used to report on it, such as earned run average, batting average, hits, and errors, were well established.

The game and its stats changed very little through most of the 20th century. Baseball became bound to its traditions. Ideas about how the game is played—and recorded and talked about—became cemented in place. Batting average was considered the most important hitting stat even though it has clear limitations.

Batting average, for example, doesn't tell anything about a hitter's power. It doesn't fully show his ability to get on base. Similarly, pitcher wins were considered the best way to judge a hurler despite obvious blind spots. Clearly, a pitcher's number of wins depends on his fielders doing their job well and his team's offense scoring runs.

◀ Joe Carter played in all 162 games for the 1990 Padres, which likely helped inflate his RBI total. He later joined the Blue Jays and became a legend after whacking a World Series-winning HR in 1993.

Runs batted in (RBI) were first recorded in 1920 as a way of recognizing the players who powered their team's offense. Even today it remains a virtually sacred stat among baseball traditionalists. But many people in baseball understand that RBIs are more of a team stat. Other hitters must get on base before anyone can knock them in. The only other way to get an RBI is to hit a solo home run.

History provides countless examples of huge RBI totals for hitters who weren't really great "run producers." Keith Law, in his book *Smart Baseball*, illustrates one glaring example. In 1990, San Diego Padres outfielder Joe Carter had a lowly .232 batting average and a miserable .290 on-base percentage. As a batter, Carter made more outs than any other batter in the National League that year. But he had 115 RBI, third most in the league.

He was able to rack up this RBI total for a couple reasons. For one, he came to the plate 697 times. That was more than all but one other player in the league. And he had 542 runners on base in front of him, the most in the league—by a lot. The player with the next-highest total had 496 base runners. The fact that Carter drove in only 115 runs actually looks puny when compared to those 542 base runners.

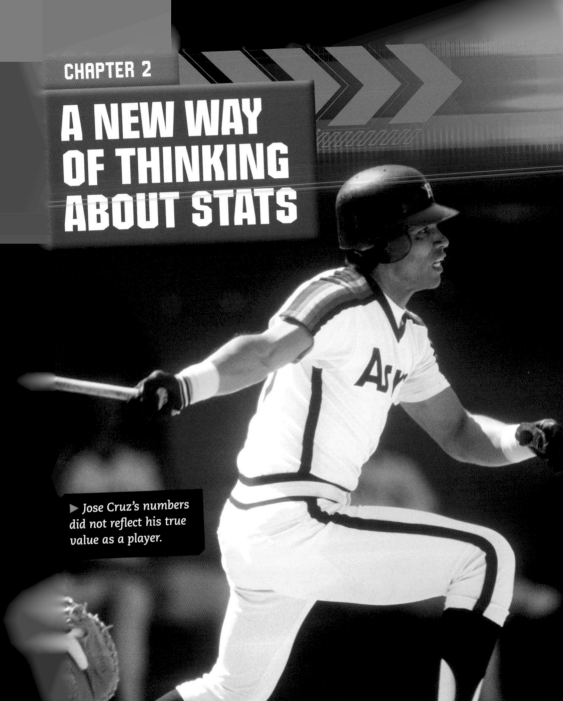

CHAPTER 2

A NEW WAY OF THINKING ABOUT STATS

▶ Jose Cruz's numbers did not reflect his true value as a player.

In baseball, the context of statistics is very important. Context refers to the conditions a player plays in. For example, it's harder to hit a home run in April, when the weather is cool, than it is in August, when warm air helps the ball carry farther. It was harder to hit home runs in the 1960s, for various reasons, than it was in the 1990s. Numbers mean a lot more if you can account for their context. Today that is a basic principle of good analysis, but people didn't always understand it.

Consider Jose Cruz, a former Houston Astros outfielder. He played for the team from 1975 to 1987 and is still one of the most popular Astros ever. Most Major League Baseball (MLB) baseball fans considered him above average. They didn't think he was one of the game's greats. His statistics bear that out. In 1980, for example, he hit .302 with 91 RBIs and 36 stolen bases. He had 185 hits that year.

When people talk about the biggest stars of that era, most don't mention Cruz. He was not in the top 10 for batting average in 1980. George Brett of the Kansas City Royals topped that list by hitting .390. Cruz was not in the top 10 for RBI. Cecil Cooper of the Milwaukee Brewers led baseball with 122. Cruz's home run total of 11 looked pitiful next to the 48 hit by Mike Schmidt of the Philadelphia Phillies.

But according to a baseball writer named Bill James, Jose Cruz was every bit as good as the best hitters of his era. The reason? Context.

Specifically, the context of home ballpark. The Houston Astrodome, where Cruz played half his games, was absolutely the worst park for hitters at that time. To adjust for context, James compared several players' batting statistics compiled only on the road. He found that Cruz was better than George Brett and other greats of the time like Dale Murphy and Jim Rice. But only on the road. George Brett played home games in Royals Stadium, one of the best hitter's parks. Dale Murphy's home park in Atlanta was equally friendly to offense. So was Jim Rice's home field—Fenway Park in Boston.

▶ *George Brett won AL batting titles in 1976, 1980, and 1990.*

When Cruz hit at home, he lost 30 points off his batting average and most of his home run power. It wasn't just Cruz. The Astrodome reduced all scoring by about 8 percent. That was mostly because its outfield fences were far away, making it significantly harder to hit home runs.

Bill James lamented that most fans never appreciated how great Cruz really was. As James said, "Cruz's statistics have defrauded him."

Society for American Baseball Research

Bill James was one of a handful of writers and baseball analysts who challenged the old ways of looking at the sport. The beginning of this small movement can be traced back to 1971. That was when a journalist and historian named L. Robert "Bob" Davids assembled a

▲ Bill James was hired as a Red Sox advisor in 2003.

group of 16 people interested in baseball, baseball analysis, and baseball research. They called themselves the Society for American Baseball Research (SABR). Their purpose was to present to one another their research and produce a publication of that research.

The first *Baseball Research Journal* came out in 1972 with several articles by Davids and others. One article by John C. Tattersall examined an old home run record. Could this old record be trusted? Tattersall asked, "Have you ever wondered about the 27 homers Ned Williamson hit for the Chicago White Stockings in 1884?"

Probably very few of his readers had wondered about that. But Tattersall's research into the player showed the direction that these new baseball thinkers were moving.

He explained that Williamson was not the power hitter he might seem to be: "In fact, he really was a mediocre batsman." The reason? That would be his home ballpark. In 1884, Tattersall's White Stockings played their home games in a field called Lake Park. According to Tattersall's research, the stadium probably had a right field fence that was no more than 230 feet from home plate. That was about one-third closer than average. Williamson took great advantage.

▶ Ned Williamson of the Chicago White Stockings

In other words: Context matters.

The Baseball Abstract

Bill James was not a part of SABR, but he was doing similar work. James was an economics major who dropped out of college to pursue baseball writing. He applied the principles of economics to analyzing baseball. In 1975 he published his first article for a national journal, *Baseball Digest*.

The article explained why it is inaccurate to compare major league players in different eras without adjusting for context. Major league statistics levels change too much from decade to decade, he explained. One example he cited was the first baseman Gus Suhr of the 1930 Pittsburgh Pirates. Suhr drove in 107 runs that year. He was nowhere near the 1930 league leader in that category, who had 191. But if Suhr had that same total in 1968, he would have led the league.

James self-published his first book in 1977 by reproducing it on a photocopy machine. Its full title explained perfectly what readers would find inside. It was called the *1977 Baseball Abstract: Featuring 18 Categories of Statistical Information That You Just Can't Find Anywhere Else.* He sold a few copies for $3.50 each.

He published the Abstract again in 1978 and for 10 more years after that. In these books he debunked myths using statistics and looked for patterns that other people missed. He analyzed baseball using statistics in ways that nobody had done before. He also introduced new statistics that he invented himself. One of those was range factor, a new way of measuring defense.

James was unhappy with the use of batting average as the favored way of measuring hitters. So James invented another new stat to better measure how well a hitter does his job. He called his stat "runs created." This number gives batters credit for not only hits but also for walks, total bases, and stolen bases, and it penalizes them for being caught stealing.

Making a Case

By 1981, James's reputation had grown enough that he got profiled in *Sports Illustrated*. The writer, Daniel Okrent, was the same man who a few years earlier had invented a form of fantasy baseball called Rotisserie Baseball. Okrent had been reading James's work for years.

Despite James's growing popularity with fans, his new ideas and challenging of tradition did not take hold with those inside the game. Players, managers, executives, and mainstream reporters ignored James (if they had even heard of him) or disdained him. Old-school baseball people disliked newcomers trying to change the way things had always been done.

But there was one time someone inside the game called on James.

Before the 1981 season, Chicago White Sox pitcher Steve Trout went to salary arbitration with his team. In arbitration, the player and team present their arguments. An arbitrator then decides what the player's salary will be. What the White Sox didn't know was that Trout's agents had hired Bill James to help them make their case.

The White Sox presented Trout's win-loss record as evidence that he wasn't very good. He'd gone 9–16, so he deserved to be paid like other pitchers with lousy win-loss records. James prepared an exhibit of the win-loss records of other starting pitchers in the division. He wanted to show what their win-loss records should have been—if they all had the same fielders, ballpark, and offense.

James' exhibit showed that Trout's record didn't really reflect how well he pitched that year. Time and time again, he had been let down by his team. The White Sox played poorly in the field and didn't score many runs for him. If Trout had enjoyed average defense and offense, his record would have been 14-11.

Trout won his case against the White Sox.

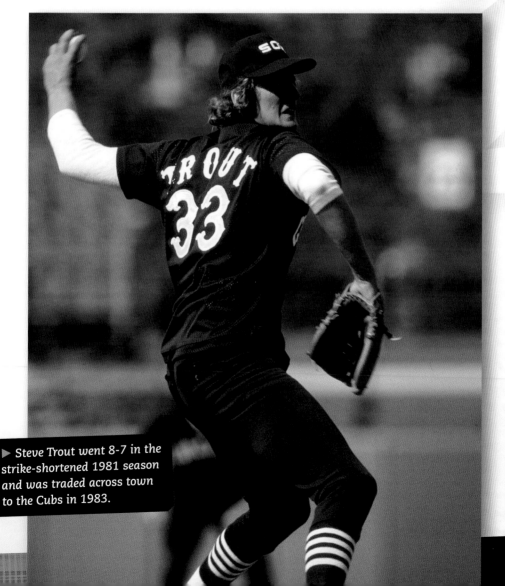

▶ Steve Trout went 8-7 in the strike-shortened 1981 season and was traded across town to the Cubs in 1983.

CHAPTER 3

SMALL CHANGES TAKE HOLD

▶ Scott Hatteberg played four seasons in Oakland during his 14 years in the major leagues.

The 2001 Oakland Athletics had a stellar starting rotation anchored by three budding superstars—Barry Zito, Tim Hudson, and Mark Mulder. They had a strong bullpen. Maybe most important of all, they had a monster lineup that terrorized opposing pitchers. First baseman Jason Giambi had won the MVP the previous year. Infielders Miguel Tejada and Eric Chavez were feared sluggers, and outfielder Johnny Damon was a rising star as a table-setter. The team won 102 games that year, but they were bounced from the playoffs in the first round by the New York Yankees.

Hopes for the next season were high in Oakland until the A's lost Giambi and Damon through free agency. Closer Jason Isringhausen signed with the Cardinals. Things did not look good. And Oakland did not have as much money to spend as most other teams—especially large-market teams like the Yankees and Red Sox.

A's general manager Billy Beane got to work replacing the players he'd lost. One of the most important moves he made was signing Scott Hatteberg to play first base. The move was disappointing to casual fans. Hatteberg was a decent hitter, but he didn't have nearly the power or batting average of Giambi, the man he was replacing. But most fans—and teams—were looking at traditional stats like batting average. Beane was looking at something else: on-base percentage.

Make an Out or Get on Base

What Beane knew, thanks to the writing of people like Bill James, was that on-base percentage (OBP) was the statistic most closely related to scoring runs. It makes sense. The basic result of every plate appearance is one of two things: You either make an out, or you get on base. If you get on base, you are not making an out. That means your team keeps on batting and keeps increasing its chances to score.

Batting average does tell us something we can use, which is how often a batter gets a hit. But getting a hit is only one way of getting on base. Another primary way is getting a walk. In the baseball world at that time, though, most people didn't think of getting walks as a batting skill. They thought of walks as mistakes made by pitchers.

▲ Billy Beane

But they were wrong. Getting walks is a skill, and Scott Hatteberg was good at it.

Because OBP was not widely acknowledged as an important statistic, teams didn't seek out players with high OBP numbers. That was important to Billy Beane. Less demand for those players meant that he could sign them for less money.

Beane made several similar moves, and his plan worked out well. Oakland's team OBP was .339, seventh best in the majors, and they scored 800 runs, which was well over the average of 747 that year. The A's won 103 games—one more than the previous season. But they were knocked out of the playoffs in the first round again, this time by the Minnesota Twins.

Gaining Attention

Sabermetrics were changing the game. Old, traditional statistics were still the most common, but newer ones were creeping into the conversation. OBP was added to player stat pages, as was slugging percentage (SLG).

Even before Billy Beane changed the way baseball teams evaluate players, the sabermetrics community had been growing. The Internet was becoming more accessible to all, and the conversation about sabermetrics flourished online. In 1996 a group of writers and statisticians formed the website *Baseball Prospectus*. The site was devoted to the kind of work Bill James and SABR had done—covering the sport mainly through statistics. While this kind of analysis is common now, at the time it was practically revolutionary.

Among the somewhat controversial points on *Baseball Prospectus* was the argument that giving away outs is a bad idea. Teams should almost never give them away on purpose. So bunting to move up a runner should rarely, if ever, be done. Yet sacrifice bunts have been a tradition for a hundred years, and few in the game paid attention. The 2005 champion White Sox had eight sacrifice bunts in the postseason alone. But baseball is changing fast. In 2016 the Red Sox had eight sacrifices all year.

In 2001, Voros McCracken published an article on *Baseball Prospectus* that turned out to be one of the most influential pieces of baseball analysis in a generation. The article was called "Pitching and Defense, How Much Control Do Hurlers Have?" In it, McCracken showed that pitchers can't control whether batted balls are turned into outs. This flew in the face of established baseball thinking, which held that good pitchers can induce weak contact or poorly hit balls. Balls like that are more easily converted to outs by his defense. But McCracken proved that it just wasn't true. So, looking at how many hits—or how many runs—a pitcher gives up does not give a totally accurate picture of his ability. So much of offense is out of the pitcher's control.

To help give a more accurate picture of a pitcher's ability, McCracken created a new statistic, defense independent pitching stats (DIPS). DIPS looks only at the things a pitcher can control: walks, strikeouts, home runs, and hit batsmen. DIPS is the result of a complex formula

McCracken created. The formula spits out a number that looks like earned run average (ERA).

▲ Ervin Santana led the American League with five shutouts in 2017.

What DIPS does, essentially, is tell us what a pitcher would do if he played with a league average defense and in a league average ballpark. Over the years, new, more refined formulas have been established for evaluating pitching without the influence of defense. One is fielding independent pitching (FIP). But the main idea remains the same. To get a truly accurate picture of a pitcher's ability, look at his fielding-independent numbers rather than his ERA. In other words, put the player's performance in neutral context.

Minnesota Twins pitcher Ervin Santana provides a useful case study. In 2016, his ERA was 3.38, but his FIP was 3.81, indicating that some combination of defense, ballpark, and luck helped him some. But in 2017, his ERA was a tidy 3.28 as he anchored the Twins' rotation and

▲ Byron Buxton won a Gold Glove for his play in 2017 in center field and helped his pitchers by making many dazzling catches.

helped lead them to a wild card berth. Santana made the All Star team that year and even got a few votes for Cy Young (coming in seventh).

But Santana actually pitched worse in 2017 than he did in 2016, according to his FIP, which was 4.46. That's 1.18 runs per game more than his ERA.

So what happened between 2016 and 2017? The Twins defense became one of the best in the league. The previous year they had Miguel Sano, a relatively slow infielder, playing right field for much of the year. They replaced him with Max Kepler, an above average fielder. And Byron Buxton, perhaps the best defensive centerfielder in the game, played only 92 games in the big leagues in 2016. But he played all of 2017, having a massive impact on defense. The Twins also improved at catcher and in the infield. Advanced statistics peg the Twins as having the third best defense in the MLB in 2017. They had been among the worst in 2016.

CALCULATING OBP AND SLG

On-base percentage is a measure of how good a hitter is at getting on base by any method. Here's the formula:

(Hits + Walks + times HBP) ÷ (AB + Walks + times HBP + Sacrifice Flies) = OBP

OBP is a great stat for evaluating a hitter's ability because it looks at two of the three most important things he does: get hits and get walks. The third most important thing is power, and that's measured with slugging percentage. SLG is simple to calculate; it's just total bases divided by total at bats. (A single is one base, a double is two bases, a triple is three, and a home run is four.)

Total Bases ÷ AB = SLG

CHAPTER 4

ADVANCED STATISTICS GO MAINSTREAM

▲ Boston celebrated a championship in 2004—the club's first since Babe Ruth was a young star for the Red Sox in the 1910s.

Baseball analysis in the 2000s was changing—slowly. But mainstream journalists, announcers, and team executives still mostly ignored the changes. Many, like TV announcer Joe Morgan, derided these new analysts as outsiders and "numbers geeks."

But not everyone in the game's establishment felt this way. One team that was ready to change was the Boston Red Sox. The Sox were in the midst of their famous title drought. They hadn't won a World Series since 1918. When they hired Theo Epstein as their general manager before the 2003 season, Epstein was only 29 years old. That made him the youngest general manager in MLB history. But the owners of the Red Sox liked his advanced analytical approach.

Like Billy Beane, Epstein was good at using stats to identify undervalued talent. He picked up high-OBP players like Kevin Millar and Bill Meuller. When the Twins released the disappointing David Ortiz after six so-so years, Epstein signed him for a song. And he hired the sabermetric-minded Terry Francona as his manager.

In the fall of 2004, the Red Sox faced a 0–3 deficit against the rival Yankees in the American League Championship Series. Over the final four games, Boston dramatically improved its on-base performance. In the first three games, all losses, they walked only five times. In the final four, all wins, they walked 23 times. David Ortiz hit three home runs in the series and was named its MVP. Oh, and he got on base at an amazing .457 clip.

After the dramatic defeat of the Yankees, Boston went on to sweep the St. Louis Cardinals in the World Series. Epstein had ended Boston's championship drought.

Going to WAR

OBP and SLG are two of the more important stats. But there are now dozens of statistics that can help shed light on what works and what

▶ Theo Epstein brought a new approach to Boston.

doesn't—and what might work in the future. Predicting player performance is a huge part of sabermetrics.

Statisticians have worked hard to find a statistic that effectively captures everything about a player's contributions. That means hitting, base running, fielding, and (when applicable) pitching. One of the most successful stats created for this purpose is wins above replacement (WAR).

WAR offers an answer to the question of what effect losing a certain player would have on the team. The stats assumes the player would be replaced by a freely available minor leaguer or bench-quality backup (a "replacement player"). The statistic is expressed in a number of wins.

For example, if a player is worth 4.4 WAR, his team would lose about 4.4 more games that season if they had a replacement player in his place. Though WAR is calculated to the decimal, it is not meant to be taken as a precise figure. It's an estimate.

WAR is often cited when people talk about MVP Awards. In 2013, for example, first baseman Miguel Cabrera of the Detroit Tigers had a monster year offensively. He had a .442 OBP and a .636 SLG. Meanwhile, Angels outfielder Mike Trout also had a great year at the plate—but not as great. His OBP was .432 and his SLG was .557.

▼ Miguel Cabrera

But those numbers didn't say anything about defense. Mike Trout was an elite fielder at one of the toughest positions, centerfield. Cabrera was a mediocre fielder at the easiest position, first base. Trout was so much more valuable than Cabrera with the glove that his WAR showed him to be the much more valuable player overall.

Trout's WAR was 9.3, the highest in all of baseball. Cabrera's was 7.3—still fantastic, but a solid two wins below Trout.

In the end, the MVP voters were not quite ready to fully embrace sabermetrics. They voted Cabrera MVP.

2013 WINS ABOVE REPLACEMENT (WAR)

	PLAYER	POSITION	TEAM	WAR
1	Mike Trout	CF	Angels	9.3
2	Carlos Gomez	CF	Brewers	8.5
3	Clayton Kershaw	P	Dodgers	8.4
4	Andrew McCutchen	CF	Pirates	8.1
5	Robinson Can	2B	Yankees	7.8
6	Josh Donaldson	3B	Athletics	7.7
7	Cliff Lee	P	Phillies	7.6
8	Miguel Cabrera	1B	Tigers	7.3
9	Paul Goldschmidt	1B	Diamondbacks	7.1
10	Andrelton Simmons	SS	Braves	7.0

Getting Shifty

Even casual fans can see one obvious change that sabermetrics has brought to MLB games—defensive shifts. Sometimes data shows that a hitter tends to pull the ball on the ground most of the time. In those cases, many managers now have their infield defense shift dramatically to that side of the field.

If you happen to be watching a game and left-handed batter Kyle Seager of the Seattle Mariners comes up, there's a good chance you'll see a shift. The shortstop and even the third baseman will probably be in ready position on the right side of the infield. With them on that side will be the second baseman and the first baseman. This shift leaves the left side of the infield totally empty. But the data shows that Seager is very unlikely to hit it to that side. It's a risk that teams are willing to take most of the time. Seager faced defensive shifts in 369 out of his 650 plate appearances in 2017.

▲ Mike Trout

Shifts have been trending up. MLB teams used the shift 2,350 times in 2011. In 2016 they used it 28,130 times. It's still unclear how effective the shift is, but teams clearly believe it works.

Sabermetrics in the World Series

The World Series in 2016 was one of the most exciting in recent years. One reason was because the Chicago Cubs were trying to break the "Curse of the Billy Goat," their 107-year title drought. The Series also featured two teams, in the Cubs and Cleveland Indians, that were among the most focused on sabermetrics.

The executive in charge of pulling the Cubs team together was Theo Epstein. He was the general manager

▲ Ben Zobrist helped carry the Cubs to the 2016 championship, thanks in part to Theo Epstein's tactics in the front office.

when Boston's title drought ended a few years earlier. The Cubs' manager was Joe Maddon. He was known as one of the most stat-driven managers in the game. As for Cleveland, they too were led by a stat-savvy front office. Their manager, Terry Francona, had been Boston's manager when Epstein was in charge there.

One of the most visible signs of Francona's sabermetric bent was how he used his pitching staff. Due to injuries, he had only one truly trustworthy starting pitcher, Corey Kluber. He also had two shutdown relievers, Andrew Miller and Cody Allen. Traditional baseball strategy is to push starters to gobble as many innings as possible. But Francona ignored tradition. Instead, knowing that every out is valuable, he went to his bullpen early and often. Andrew Miller came into games as early as the fifth inning. Kluber, Miller, and Allen ended up pitching more than half of Cleveland's postseason innings.

The Cubs on the other hand were a model of OBP and defensive excellence. Epstein had focused on collecting players strong in OBP, defense, and positional versatility. Ben Zobrist provided the perfect model of this approach. "Zorilla" had a low batting average. So he was undervalued by traditional standards. But he played excellent D and played all over the field. He also got on base at a high rate. It was fitting that he hit the double that gave the Cubs their Series-clinching lead.

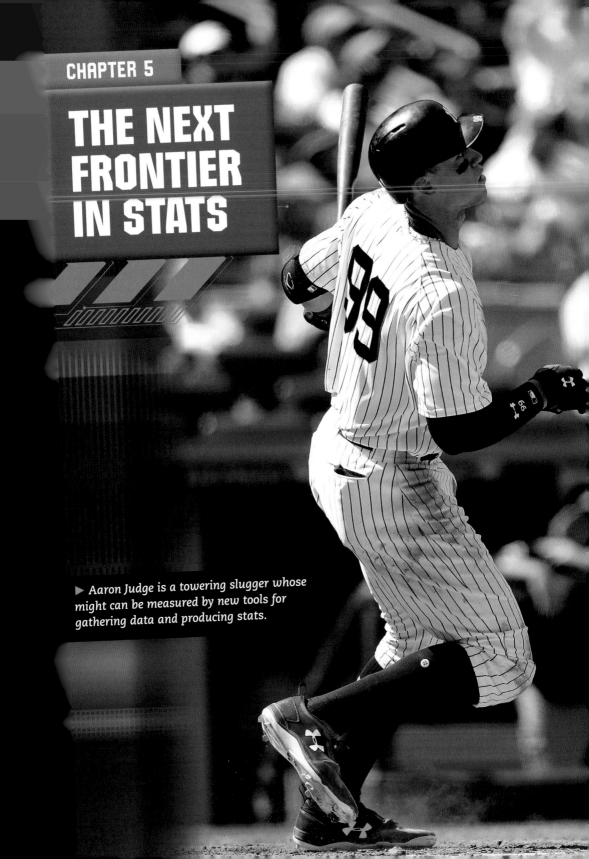

CHAPTER 5

THE NEXT FRONTIER IN STATS

▶ Aaron Judge is a towering slugger whose might can be measured by new tools for gathering data and producing stats.

Yankees rookie Aaron Judge came up to bat in the first inning of a June 2017 game. He faced Chris Tillman of the Orioles. On a 1-0 pitch, he took a mighty swing at a meatball down the middle. The ball left his bat at a 25-degree angle and screamed away at 121.1 miles per hour. It stayed just inside the foul pole for a home run.

It was more than just another home run for Judge, who would hit 52 of them that year. It was the hardest hit ball by anyone all year. In fact it was the hardest hit ball in at least three years. It was topped on the last day of the season when the Miami Marlins' Giancarlo Stanton smacked a single that reached 122.2 miles per hour.

The reason we know that is because of MLB's Statcast tracking technology. Statcast is the new big thing in baseball analytics. Every major-league ballpark is now equipped with high-powered cameras and radar equipment. These precisely track the location and movements of the ball, from the moment it leaves the pitcher's hand until the play is over. The technology also tracks everyone on the field—every fielder, base runner, coach, and umpire.

Statcast has only been around since 2015, so its full impact is yet to be known. But already it has changed the game. For one thing, home runs have spiked. In 2014, which was the season before Statcast, MLB players hit 4,186 home runs. That was down a bit from previous years, but the total has mostly been between 4,000 and 5,000 since the league started testing for steroids in 2003.

In 2015, when teams began to have access to Statcast data, there were 4,909 home runs hit. In 2016 the total was 5,610. And in 2017 big-league players cranked 6,105. That was the highest total in the history of the MLB by more than 400 bombs.

What's happening? Players and coaches were analyzing hit data obtained from Statcast. From that, they were learning the best launch angle for hitting more home runs. Then players trained themselves to change their swings so that they would make contact at that launch angle.

Washington Nationals second baseman Daniel Murphy provided a shining example of this. In 2015, while with the Mets, he began to change his approach at the plate. He moved closer to the plate and reduced the gap between his elbows. This led to a higher launch angle on his batted balls. The results are clear. His average launch angle was 12.1 degrees in 2015, and he had a SLG of .449. In 2016 his average launch angle was 16.9 degrees, and his SLG jumped to .595. He hit 25 homers (up from 14).

All About the Data

Baseball analysis typically tries to put a value on a player or an action, often by measuring how many runs or wins it's worth. With Statcast, we can see exactly how a play happened, why it happened, and what its value was.

Statcast tells us the pitcher's release point. It tells us how much time passes from the pitcher's first movement until the ball crosses the plate. The system lets us know not only how fast the pitch was, but also how fast it looked to the hitter. We can find out how fast the ball travels off a player's bat. We can know the launch angle, hang time, and distance of batted balls.

Defense has always been the hardest part of the game for analysts to measure with statistics. But Statcast is casting new light on that area too. Ever wonder how fast centerfielder Billy Hamilton of the Cincinnati Reds ran

SPRINT SPEED (2017)

RANK	PLAYER	POSITION	AGE	SPRINT SPEED (FT / SEC)
1	Byron Buxton	CF	24	30.2
2	Billy Hamilton	CF	27	30.1
3	Bradley Zimmer	CF	25	29.9
4	Dee Gordon	2B	29	29.7
5	Amed Rosario	SS	22	29.7

to make an amazing catch? Statcast has data on the acceleration and top speed ("sprint speed") of defenders as well as base runners. It has data explaining the efficiency of a fielder's route to the ball. It tells us the probability of any batted ball being caught, and it also gives us the velocity of a fielder's throw.

Teams had access to some Statcast data even earlier than 2015, and they've been finding ways to use it to their advantage. In 2013 the Astros picked up pitcher Collin McHugh off waivers from the Rockies. The right-hander had pitched in only 15 major league games, and things hadn't gone well. He had an 8.94 ERA. The Astros, though, saw something they liked about McHugh in the Statcast data. The spin rate on his curveball was very good. The Astros coached him to throw the pitch more, and the results were stark. He threw 154.2 innings in 2014 with an ERA of 2.73. To use a more advanced stat, he earned 4.2 WAR.

The Age of Analytics

Today, all 30 MLB teams recognize the value of analyzing data, and all 30 have a robust analytics department. You can't compete in today's game without a deep commitment to analytics.

We can see the results of this analytic age in the game we see on the field. Bunts are way down because teams understand that they often don't pay off. Stolen base attempts are down too—the numbers show that it's

▲ Speedy Billy Hamilton
of the Cincinnati Reds

not worth risking an out. Strikeouts and home runs are
way up as teams coach hitters to focus on power. And
teams are looking for pitchers with the ability to strike
batters out more than ever because they know that they
can't control what happens to balls in play. Walks are up,
too, as more teams value OBP. Managers use more relief
pitchers, and they use them earlier in games.

Teams are smarter than ever at finding ways to win. But games are getting longer. More walks and strikeouts means more pitches thrown and longer at-bats. Add more home runs to the mix, and we have longer games and far fewer balls in play. Home runs are fun, and strikeouts can be exciting. But fans also love to see great defensive plays. Fans want to

▶ Fielding whiz
Andrelton Simmons
of the Angels

see Andrelton Simmons making a backhand grab in the hole and firing to first, just nipping a speedy runner. They want to see Lorenzo Cain galloping across the outfield to snare what seemed like a sure hit. Fans love to see action. Maybe the next revolution in stats will bring more of it back into the game.

One area where there's still plenty of progress to be made is in player health. Teams' medical and training departments have lots of data at their disposal too. They're looking for better ways to predict, prevent, and treat injuries. For example, if a pitcher's spin rate decreases, it could be an indication that he's fatigued—and thus more likely to get hurt. A team can give him ample rest before he gets hurt.

We probably won't see another team like the Athletics and Red Sox of the mid-2000s that gains a huge advantage through analytics. Statcast is available to everyone, and it has leveled the playing field in a big way. But advantages are still there to be found, and teams are hiring more analysts to find them. Those advantages aren't likely to be as big as they once were, but they are there—in the numbers. The statheads have taken over the game, and they're here to stay.

STAT GLOSSARY

batting average (BA)—the ratio of base hits per official times at bat, expressed as a three-digit decimal

earned run average (ERA)—the average number of earned runs a pitcher gives up over nine innings; it is determined by dividing the total number of earned runs scored against him by the total number of innings pitched and multiplying by nine

fielding independent pitching (FIP)—a measure of a pitcher's effectiveness if he had an average defense behind him; by looking only at strikeouts and walks and home runs allowed—the things that a pitcher controls on his own—it computes a number that looks like ERA

on-base percentage (OBP)— a measure of how often a batter reaches base; add up the number of times a batter reaches base by hit, walk, or hit by pitch, and divide that sum by the number of times he came to the plate

runs batted in (RBI)—a run that a batter causes to score by getting a hit, out, walk, or hit by pitch

runs created—Bill James stat that attempts to give a full picture of a batter's contribution; it gives batters credit for hits, walks, total bases, and stolen bases, and it penalizes them for being caught stealing

save—awarded to a relief pitcher who completes a game that his team wins and he meets one of the following conditions: 1) He enters the game with a lead of no more than three runs and pitches for at least one inning; 2) He enters the game, regardless of the score, with the potential tying run either on base, at bat, or on deck; 3) He pitches for at least three innings

slugging percentage (SLG)—a measure of a batter's power, it is calculated as total bases divided by at bats

ultimate zone rating (UZR)—used to measure fielding, UZR compares what happens to a batted ball (hit, out, or error) to data on similarly hit balls in the past to determine how much better or worse the fielder did than the "average" player

walks plus hits per inning pitched (WHIP)—the number of base runners a pitcher allows on average per inning

wins above replacement (WAR)—a stat that attempts to answer the question of what would be the effect on a team if they lost a certain player and he was replaced by a freely available minor leaguer or bench-quality backup; the statistic, which is calculated using a complex formula, is expressed in a number of wins

READ MORE

Lyon, Drew. *Baseball's Best and Worst: A Guide to the Game's Good, Bad, and Ugly*. North Mankato, Minn.: 2018.

Martirano, Ron. *Baseball: Great Records, Weird Happenings, Odd Facts, Amazing Moments & Other Cool Stuff*. Watertown, Mass.: Imagine, 2015.

Savage, Jeff. *Baseball Super Stats*. Minneapolis: Lerner Publications, 2018.

INTERNET SITES

Use FactHound to find Internet sites related to this book.

Visit **www.facthound.com** Just type in 9781543514483 and go.

Check out projects, games and lots more at
www.capstonekids.com

INDEX

Allen, Cody, 37

Baseball Prospectus website, 25–26
Beane, Billy, 23, 24, 25
box scores, 9–10
Brach, Brad, 5
Brett, George, 15, 16
Britton, Zach, 4–5, 6
Buxton, Byron, 29, 41

Cabrera, Miguel, 33–34
Carter, Joe, 13
Chadwick, Henry, 8–9, 10–11
Chavez, Eric, 23
context, 15–16, 18, 19, 27
Cooper, Cecil, 15
Cruz, Jose, 15–16

Damon, Johnny, 23
Davids, L. Robert "Bob," 17
defense independent pitching stats
     (DIPS), 26–27

Encarnacion, Edwin, 6
Epstein, Theo, 31, 32, 36–37

fielding independent pitching (FIP), 27, 28
Francona, Terry, 31, 37

Giambi, Jason, 23

Hatteberg, Scott, 23, 24
Hudson, Tim, 23

James, Bill, 15, 16, 17, 18–19, 20–21, 24, 25
Jiminez, Ubaldo, 6
Judge, Aaron, 39

Kepler, Max, 28–29
Kluber, Corey, 37

Law, Keith, 13

Maddon, Joe, 37
McCracken, Voros, 26, 27
McHugh, Collin, 42

medical data, 45
Meuller, Bill, 31
Millar, Kevin, 31
Miller, Andrew, 37
Morgan, Joe, 31
Mulder, Mark, 23
Murphy, Dale, 16
Murphy, Daniel, 40

O'Day, Darren, 6
Okrent, Daniel, 20
on-base percentage (OBP), 24–25, 29, 31,
     33, 37, 43
Ortiz, David, 31–32

Rice, Jim, 16
runs batted in (RBI), 7, 13, 15
runs created, 19

sacrifice bunts, 26
Sano, Miguel, 28
Santana, Ervin, 27–28
saves, 6–7
Schmidt, Mike, 15
Seager, Kyle, 35
Showalter, Buck, 5, 6–7
slugging percentage (SLG), 25, 29, 33, 40
Society for American Baseball Research
     (SABR), 17–18, 25
Stanton, Giancarlo, 39
Statcast, 39–40, 41–42, 45
Suhr, Gus, 19

Tattersall, John C., 17–18
Tejada, Miguel, 23
Tillman, Chris, 39
Trout, Mike, 33–34
Trout, Steve, 20–21

Williamson, Ned, 17–18
wins above replacement
     (WAR), 32–34, 42

Zito, Barry, 23
Zobrist, Ben, 37